THE HEREAFTER

Theresa Flatt

Copyright 2019 byTheresa Flatt.

Published 2019.

Printed in the United States of America.

All rights reserved.

No portion of this book may be reproduced, stored in a retrieval system, or transmitted in any form or by any means – electronic, mechanical, photocopy, recording, scanning, or other – except for brief quotations in critical reviews or articles, without the prior written permission of the author.

ISBN 978-1-943650-96-5

All scriptures used throughout this book are from the King James Bible.

Published by BookCrafters, Parker, Colorado.
www.bookcrafters.net

FOREWORD

I wrote this book because of some questions I had in my mind.

In 2003, my 24-year-old nephew killed himself. It was very hard for me to deal with. Then, in 2005, my mom died from cancer.

I could not rely on what I had heard most of my life about what others said about where you went in death. So I began to search the scriptures and was amazed at what the scriptures really said.

The more I searched the more open the Word of God became. This has truly helped me, to better deal with the death of loved ones.

In no way or fashion, am I saying one is in hell and the other in heaven. Only God knows where a person will end up in eternity. But, for me, this has given me peace.

I pray that this book helps others also.

TABLE OF CONTENTS

Death...1

The Body..8

The Flesh..9

The Spirit (The Breath of Life)...10

The Soul..12

A Sinner..15

A Child of God...22

Heaven...29

A Note from the Author..39

DEATH

"To everything there is a season, and a time to every purpose under the heaven: A time to be born, and a time to die;" (Ecclesiastes 3:1-2)

EVERY PERSON ON THE FACE OF THE EARTH is born to die. It does not matter if you are young or old, rich or poor, healthy or sickly we are all going to die. Only God knows exactly when each of us will die.

The real question here is, "What really takes place in death the very moment a person dies?"

On any given day you can ask someone who has lost a loved one in death, where that person is, and the answer is always, that they are in heaven. Is it possible that everyone goes to heaven, and do they really go immediately at death?

I have heard all my life that loved ones are in heaven watching down over us, to some degree. But, the scriptures say something totally opposite of what we hear.

So let's see what the Word of God has to say what happens to a person at death.

"And when thy days be fulfilled, and thou shalt sleep with thy fathers," (2 Samuel 7:12)

"So David slept with his fathers, and was buried in the city of David." (1 Kings 2:10)

"And Solomon slept with his fathers, and was buried in the city of David his father: (1 Kings 11:43)

"And Jehoshaphat slept with his fathers, and was buried with his fathers in the city of David his father: (1 Kings 22:50)

So, it's pretty clear to see that when a person died, it was said that they slept.

"Consider and hear me, O Lord my God: lighten my eyes, lest I sleep the sleep of death;" (Psalms 13:3)

"And there shall be no night there; and they need no candle, neither light of the sun; for the Lord God giveth them light: and they shall reign for ever and ever." (Revelation 22:5)

So if they slept, it's reasonable to understand that they are in the grave, and not in heaven. Being that there is no night time in heaven, you will not be sleeping.

"For in death there is no remembrance of thee: in the grave who shall give these thanks?" (Psalms 6:5)

If a person in the grave does not even remember to praise God, you can be assured he is not going to remember his loved ones.

> *"Whatsoever thy hand findeth to do, do it with thy might; for there is no work, nor device, nor knowledge, nor wisdom, in the grave, wither thou goest."* (Ecclesiastes 9:10)

So here again we see that the grave can be a place of total peace. So, that loved ones cannot be looking down over us, according to the scriptures. Does this mean that every person who has died is at peace in the grave?

Let's now look in the New Testament.

> *"And he kneeled down, and cried with a loud voice, Lord, lay not this sin to their charge. And when he had said this, he fell asleep."* (Acts 7:60)

> *"These things said he: and after that he saith unto them, Our friend Lazarus sleepeth; but I go, that I may awake him out of sleep."* (John 11:11)

Jesus knew Lazarus was dead, but he was to raise him up again from that sleep. He did not call Lazarus to come down from heaven, but to come forth from the grave.

> *"And it came to pass, that the beggar died, and was carried by the angels into Abraham's bosom: the rich man also died, and was buried;"* (Luke 16:22)

"And in hell he lift up his eyes, being in torments, and seeth Abraham afar off, and Lazarus in his bosom." (Luke 16:23)

Now let's look at this very closely. The rich man was in hell being in torments. He could see Lazarus, he could feel pain, and he even remembers his brothers. So that let's me know he is not at peace of any kind. This tells me he died a sinner.

But, notice what it does not say here about Lazarus. No where does it say that Lazarus saw the rich man, he does not even hear him talking to Abraham. Why? Because, Lazarus is asleep in death, he is in total peace. He hears nothing, sees nothing, feels nothing, and remembers nothing.

But, the rich man on the other hand, feels all pain, sees the graves of the saints, and the worst of all, remembers the past. That tells me he remembers all the chances he had to become a child of God, and didn't take the opportunity to live for God, but chose to stay a sinner.

And he cried and said, Father Abraham, have mercy on me, and send Lazarus, that he may dip the tip of his finger in water, and cool my tongue; for I am tormented in this flame." (Luke 16:24)

"But Abraham said, Son, remember that thou in thy lifetime receivedst thy good things, and likewise Lazarus evil things: but now he is comforted, and thou art tormented." (Luke 16:25)

Lazarus is comforted, in a peaceful sleep, while the rich man is tormented and in flames, and has his memory.

"And beside all this, between us and you there is a great gulf fixed: so that they which would pass from hence to you cannot; neither can they pass to us, that would come from thence." (Luke 16:26)

Nowhere do the scriptures say that Lazarus is in heaven, only that a great gulf is between them. And that gulf keeps them from crossing to the other one.

I believe a sinner can be right next to a child of God in the ground and the child of God not even knows they are there, but the sinner will see them as though they are a way from them. That gulf completely separates them, from being able to touch or talk to the other.

"So man lieth down, and riseth not: till the heavens be no more, they shall not awake, nor be raised out of their sleep." (Job 14:12)

So let's get back to the New Testament.

"And, behold, the veil of the temple was rent in twain from the top to the bottom; and the earth did quake, and the rocks rent;" (Matthew 27:51)

"And the graves were opened; and many bodies of the saints which slept arose," (Matthew 27:52)

> *"And came out of the graves after his resurrection, and went into the holy city, and appeared unto many."* (Matthew 27:53)

Wow! Can you just imagine, seeing the dead come back walking around? Here again, he did not call them down from heaven, they came forth from the grave. No sinners came back, only some of the saints.

> *"And many of them that sleep in the dust of the earth shall awake, some to everlasting life, some to shame and everlasting contempt."* (Daniel 12:2)

> *"Verily, verily, I say unto you, The hour is coming, and now is, when the dead shall hear the voice of the Son of God: and they that hear shall live."* (John 5:25)

A lot of people think that a person can die a sinner and be saved after death, but this is opposite of what the Bible says.

> *"For the grave cannot praise thee, death cannot celebrate thee: they that go down into the pit cannot hope for thy truth."* (Isaiah 38:18)

> *"But if our gospel be hid, it is hid to them that are lost:"* (2 Corinthians 4:3)

It gets no clearer than this, if you die a sinner you have no hope of ever finding God again. God gives us a lifetime to find him, and we make our own choices. Nobody can make you live for God. God will not make you serve him, it is your choice, and therefore God does not send anyone to hell. If a person ends up in hell, it is because that person chose to go there, by not choosing to live for God.

Now that we know everyone has a choice in where he spends eternity, just what exactly happens to the whole body itself when you die?

THE BODY

"And the Lord God formed man of the dust of the ground, and breathed into his nostrils the breath of life; and man became a living soul." (Genesis 2:7)

THE SCRIPTURES SAY that a person is made up of three parts: the flesh, the breath of life or spirit, and the soul.

Let's look at each part to see what happens to each separately at the time a person dies.

THE FLESH

THE FLESH IS THE VERY FIRST part God created. He formed the flesh from nothing more that the dirt from the ground. So, just what happens to our flesh in death?

> *"In the sweat of thy face shalt thou eat bread, till thou return unto the ground; for out of it wast thou taken: for dust thou art, and unto dust shalt thou return."* (Genesis 3:19)

> *"All flesh shall perish together, and man shall turn again unto dust."* (Job 34:15)

> *"All go unto one place; all are of the dust, and all turn to dust again."* (Ecclesiastes 3:20)

The scriptures are very clear as to what happens to our flesh, it will return to the dust that it was taken from.

THE SPIRIT
(The Breath of Life)

THE SECOND PART OF THE BODY is the spirit, or breath of life. God breathed into man the spirit that is life. That is the only way we can live is because of Him breathing life into us.

> *"The Spirit of God hath made me, and the breath of the Almighty hath given me life."* (Job 33:4)

> *"For as the body without the spirit is dead, so faith without works is dead also."* (James 2:26)

> *"Then shall the dust return to the earth as it was: and the spirit shall return unto God who gave it."* (Ecclesiastes 12:7)

The scriptures clearly say what happens to the spirit or the breath of life once a person dies. Our spirit does not stay with us in death, it clearly returns back to our Creator.

Because I now have this understanding, things I have heard about most of my life, now makes sense. I have heard and read stories of where people have seen their loved ones, leave their bodies, going to heaven.

I know a man that was with his friend, when the friend died, and felt the person go through his body to heaven. I understand now, that it was not their soul, it was their spirit returning to its Creator.

No matter who you are, a sinner or a child of God, that spirit returns unto God. So does this mean they are in heaven? No. Only their spirit returned unto God.

THE SOUL

THE THIRD AND LAST PART of the body is the soul. This by far, is the most important part of man, because, this is the part that lives through eternity somewhere.

> *"And fear not them which kill the body, but are not able to kill the soul: but rather fear him which is able to destroy both soul and body in hell."* (Matthew 10:28)

> *"And as it is appointed unto men once to die, but after this the judgment:"* (Hebrews 9:27)

Everyone on the face of the earth will stand before God, and be judged by His word.

> *"And I saw the dead, small and great, stand before God; and the books were opened: and another book was opened, which is the book of life: and the dead were judged out of those things which were written in the books, according to their works."* (Revelation 20:12)

It is interesting to note here that there are the books, and a book. The single book is the one you want your name in, and the books are very simply the Word of God. The Bible has 66 books in it, and you can be assured that we will be judged by every word that is in the Bible.

"In the beginning was the Word, and the Word was with God, and the Word was God." (John 1:1)

This scripture alone tells us just how important the Bible is. So, depending on the state our soul is in at death, will determine where we spend eternity.

We are either a sinner or a child of God, there are no other choices. We have a choice as to how we live our lives.

"And if it seem evil unto you to serve the Lord, choose you this day whom you will serve; whether the gods which your fathers served that were on the other side of the flood, or the gods of the Amorites, in whose land ye dwell: but as for me and my house, we will serve the Lord." (Joshua 24:15)

"No man can serve two masters: for either he will hate the one, and love the other; or else he will hold to the one, and despise the other. Ye cannot serve God and mammon." (Matthew 6:24)

"Jesus said unto him, Thou shalt love the Lord thy God with all thy heart, and with all thy soul, and with all thy mind." (Matthew 22:37)

Our soul has a destination in eternity. It's up to each person individually where his soul spends eternity. Heaven or hell, there is no other choice.

A SINNER

"And if it seem evil unto you to serve the Lord, choose you this day whom you will serve; whether the gods which your fathers served that were on the other side of the flood, or the gods of the Amorites, in whose land ye dwell: but as for me and my house, we will serve the Lord." (Joshua 24:15)

EVERY SINGLE PERSON on the earth has to make this choice for themselves. Who are you going to serve, God or Satan? That is the only two choices you have. When we chose to live our lives our way, we are choosing not to serve God.

"No man can serve two masters: for either he will hate the one, and love the other; or else he will hold to the one, and despise the other. Ye cannot serve God and mammon." (Matthew 6:24)

A sinner's only happiness is what he enjoyed on this earth. Because once he dies, all joy, peace, or any happiness is gone.

> *"For the grave cannot praise thee, death can not celebrate thee: they that go down into the pit cannot hope for the truth."* (Isaiah 38:18)

Here again, this verse is reminding us, that once you die, there is no hope of ever being saved. That is a hard truth, but the fact is you chose where you spend eternity. God does not send anyone to hell, we send ourselves.

> *"Enter ye in at the strait gate: for wide is the gate, and broad is the way, that leadeth to destruction, and many there be which go in thereat:"* (Matthew 7:13)

> *"Because strait is the gate, and narrow is the way, which leadeth unto life, and few there be that find it."* (Matthew 7:14)

> *"Therefore hell hath enlarged herself, and opened her mouth without measure: and their glory, and their multitude, and their pomp, and he that rejoiceth, shall decend into it."* (Isiah 5:14)

> *"And many of them that sleep in the dust of the earth shall awake, some to everlasting life, and some to shame and everlasting contempt."* (Daniel 12:2)

> *"And in hell he lift up his eyes, being in torments, and seeth Abraham afar off, and Lazarus in his bosom."* (Luke 16:23)

As soon as a sinner dies, their soul is in torments in the grave. They feel all pain, hear, and see. How awful to remember your life as it was, and realize every opportunity you had to choose God, but didn't. You have to stand before God and be judged by every word that is in the Bible with no excuse. You had your whole life to choose God, but still didn't. Then, after you are judged, you are cast into outer darkness with the devil and his angels for eternity.

"And then will I profess unto them, I never knew you: depart from me, ye that work iniquity." (Matthew 7:23)

"I charge thee therefore before God, and the Lord Jesus Christ, who shall judge the quick and the dead at his appearing and his kingdom;" (2 Timothy 4:1)

"And as it is appointed unto men once to die, but after this the judgment:" (Hebrews 9:27)

"And I saw the dead, small and great, stand before God; and the books were opened: and another book was opened, which is the book of life: and the dead were judged out of those things which were written in the books, according to their works." (Revelation 20:12)

"And the sea gave up the dead which were in it; and death and hell delivered up the dead which were in them: and they were judged every man according to their works." (Revelation 20:13)

"And death and hell were cast into the lake of fire. This is the second death." (Revelation 20:14)

"And whosoever was not found written in the book of life was cast into the lake of fire." (Revelation 20:15)

"And shall cast them into a furnace of fire: there shall be wailing and gnashing of teeth." (Matthew 13:42)

"Where their worm dieth not, and the fire is not quenched." (Mark 9:48)

"But I will forewarn you whom ye shall fear: Fear him, which after he hath killed hath power to cast into hell; yea, I say unto you, Fear him." (Luke 12:5)

"Upon the wicked he shall rain snares, fire and brimstone, and an horrible tempest: this shall be the portion of their cup." (Psalms 11:6)

"Let burning coals fall upon them: let them be cast into the fire; into deep pits, that they rise not up again." (Psalms 140:10)

"And shall cut him asunder, and appoint him his portion with the hypocrites: there shall be weeping and gnashing of teeth." (Matthew 24:51)

"And these shall go away into everlasting punishment: but the righteous into life eternal." (Matthew 25:46)

"In flaming fire taking vengeance on them that know not God, and that obey not the gospel of our Lord Jesus Christ:" (2 Thessalonians 1:8)

"Who shall be punished with everlasting destruction from the presence of the Lord, and from the glory of his power;" (2 Thessalonians 1:9)

" For if God spared not the angels that sinned, but cast them down to hell, and delivered them into chains of darkness, to be reserved unto judgment;" (2 Peter 2:4)

"And spared not the old world, but saved Noah the eighth person, a preacher of righteousness, bringing in the flood upon the world of the ungodly;" (2 Peter 2:5)

"And turning the cities of Sodom and Gomorrah into ashes condemned them with an overthrow, making them an ensample unto those that after should live ungodly;" (2 Peter 2:6)

"And delivered just Lot, vexed with the filthy conversation of the wicked:" (2 Peter 2:7)

"(For that righteous man dwelling among them, in seeing and hearing, vexed his righteous soul from day to day with their unlawful deeds;)" (2 Peter 2:8)

"The Lord knoweth how to deliver the godly out of temptations, and to reserve the unjust unto the day of judgment to be punished:" (2 Peter 2:9)

"But the heavens and the earth, which are now, by the same word are kept in store, reserved unto fire against the day of judgment and perdition of ungodly men." (2 Peter 3:7)

"Even as Sodom and Gomorrah, and the cities about them in like manner, giving themselves over to fornication, and going after strange flesh, are set forth for an example, suffering the vengeance of eternal fire." (Jude 7)

"But the fearful, and unbelieving, and the abominable, and murders, and whoremongers, and sorcerers, and idolaters, and all liars, shall have their part in the lake which burneth with fire and brimstone: which is the second death." (Revelation 21:8)

"But if our gospel be hid, it is hid to them that are lost:" (2 Corinthians 4:3)

That scripture almost sounds cruel, but in all reality, it's not. It is our responsibility to know God. The breath of life that God gave us, that spirit, is what craves God. We either fill that longing in our spirit or we please our flesh. Again, it's our choice. All you have to do to find it is open your Bible, and allow God to open the Word to you. Each of us MUST have a personal relationship with God. That relationship is what draws us closer to him.

You will never know Him, if you only open your Bible when you go to church. A preacher can't teach you everything you need to know in a life time. You have to connect to God, by studying His word.

You will never have a personal relationship with God, if you never spend time in prayer talking to Him. You have to have prayer life every day, and I'm not talking about just 10 or 15 minutes. You have to really connect with God, before He will ever open your understanding.

How much would you know about your spouse, if you only saw them a couple of hours a week, and only talked to them in passing. I am pretty sure that very few would stay together, yet, for most of us, that's about all we give God.

So, what are you doing to prepare for eternity? Are you really giving God all you've got, or just what you want to give Him? How awful it will be to hear these words from Jesus:

"And then will I profess unto them, I never knew you: depart from me, ye worker of iniquity."
(Matthew 7:23)

The choice is yours, choose you this day whom you will serve!

A CHILD OF GOD

As in the first chapter, Death, we will look again at what happens to a child of God when they die.

"A good name is better than precious ointment; and the day of death than the day of one's birth." (Ecclesiastes 7:1)

The scriptures only hold true if you're a child of God. Only a child of God has hope of everlasting life.

"Precious in the sight of the Lord is the death of his saints." (Psalms 116:15)

"That Christ should suffer, and that he should be the first that should rise from the dead, and should shew light unto the people, and to the Gentiles." (Acts 26:23)

"Now if Christ be preached that he rose from the dead, how say some among you that there is no resurrection of the dead?" (1Corinthians 15:12)

"But if there be no resurrection of the dead, then is Christ not risen:" (1Corinthians 15:13)

"And if Christ be not risen, then is our preaching vain, and your faith is also vain." (1 Corinthians 15:14)

"Yea, and we are found false witnesses of God; because we have testified of God that he raised up Christ: whom he raised not up. If so be that the dead rise not." (1 Corinthians 15:15)

"For if the dead rise not, then is not Christ raised:" (1 Corinthians 15:16)

"And if Christ be not raised, your faith is vain; ye are yet in your sins." (1 Corinthians 15:17)

"Then they also which are fallen asleep in Christ are perished." (1 Corinthians 15:18)

Jesus had to rise from the grave before we ever could have a chance at eternal life.

"If in this life only we have hope in Christ, we are of all men most miserable." (1 Corinthians 15:19)

"But now is Christ risen from the dead, and become the first fruits of them that slept." (1Corinthians 15:20)

"For since by man came death, by man came also the resurrection of the dead." (1Corinthians 15:21)

Had Christ not risen from the dead, our hope would be nothing except death. But, Christ rose first to bring us that hope in Him.

"Behold therefore, I will gather thee unto thy fathers, and thou shalt be gathered into thy grave in peace; and thine eyes shall not see all the evil which I will bring upon this place. And they brought the king word again." (2 Kings 22:20)

"So man lieth down, and riseth not: till the heavens be no more, they shall not awake, nor be raised out of their sleep." (Job 14:12)

"For in death there is no remembrance of thee: in the grave who shall give thee thanks?" (Psalms 6:5)

"Whatsoever thy hand findeth to do, do it with thy might; for there is no work, nor device, nor knowledge, nor wisdom, in the grave, whither thou goest." (Ecclesiastes 9:10)

"And many of them that sleep in the dust of the earth shall awake, some to everlasting life, and some to shame and everlasting contempt." (Daniel 12:2)

The scriptures clearly show us that we will sleep in death before we are ever raised up.

"But God will redeem my soul from the power of the grave: for he shall receive me. Selah." (Psalms 49:15)

"I will ransom them from the power of the grave; I will redeem them from death: O death, I will be thy plagues; O grave, I will be thy destruction: repentance shall be hid from my eyes." (Hosea 13:14)

"Verily, verily, I say unto you, The hour is coming, and now is, when the dead shall hear the voice of the Son of God: and they that hear shall live." (John 5:25)

"Marvel not at this: for the hour is coming, in the which all that are in the graves shall hear his voice," (John 5:28)

"And shall come forth; they that have done good, unto the resurrection of life; and they that have done evil, unto the resurrection of damnation." (John 5:29)

"And have hope toward God, which they themselves also allow, that there shall be a resurrection of the dead, both of the just and unjust." (Acts 24:15)

"For if we have been planted together in the likeness of his death, we shall be also in the likeness of his resurrection:" (Romans 6:5)

"For the Lord himself shall descend from heaven with a shout, with the voice of the archangel, and with the trump of God: and the dead in Christ shall rise first:" (1 Thessalonians 4:16)

"Then we which are alive and remain shall be caught up together with them in the clouds, to meet the Lord in the air: and so shall we ever be with the Lord." (1 Thessalonians 4:17)

"Wherefore comfort one another with these words." (1 Thessalonians 4:18)

"Verily I say unto you, There be some standing here, which shall not taste of death, till they see the Son of man coming in his kingdom." (Matthew 16:28)

"Behold, I shew you a mystery; We shall not all sleep, but we shall all be changed," (1Corinthians 15:51)

No doubt about it, children of God have hope in the grave. We will live again. I am so glad to understand that we will be resurrected from the grave.

"The wicked is driven away in his wickedness: but the righteous hath hope in his death." (Proverbs 14:32)

"For when they shall rise from the dead, they neither marry, nor are given in marriage; but are as the angels which are in heaven." (Mark 12:25)

"And as touching the dead, that they rise: have ye not read in the book of Moses, how in the bush God spoke unto him, saying, I am the God of Abraham, and the God of Isaac, and the God of Jacob?" (Mark 12:26)

"He is not the God of the dead, but the God of the living: ye do therefore greatly err." (Mark 12:27)

"Fear none of those things which thou shalt suffer: behold, the devil shall cast some of you into prison, that ye may be tried; and ye shall have tribulation ten days: be thou faithful unto death, and I will give thee a crown of life." (Revelation 2:10)

"And I saw a new heaven and a new earth: for the first heaven and the first earth were passed away; and there was no more sea." (Revelation 21:1)

"And I John saw the holy city, new Jerusalem, coming down from God out of heaven, prepared as a bride adorned for her husband." (Revelation 21:2)

"And I heard a great voice out of heaven saying, Behold, the tabernacle of God is with men, and he will dwell with them, and they shall be his people, and God himself shall be with them, and be their God." (Revelation 21:3)

"And God shall wipe away all tears from their eyes; and there shall be no more death, neither sorrow, nor crying, neither shall there be no more pain: for the former things are passed away." (Revelation 21:4)

The scriptures clearly say what will happen to a child of God. I have been told all my life that you go to heaven as soon as you die, but, I just do not believe that, after searching all this out.

If that were true, God would literally have to send

people back to the earth to resurrect them, and I really doubt that He will do that. The scriptures clearly say that the dead in Christ will rise first and then those that are alive will meet up with them in the air. I am so glad to have more understanding on this, because I always hated the thought that people in heaven were watching over us. I knew if that was true, then heaven could not possibly be how the Bible says it is.

Imagine being in heaven and looking down over earth. You would see every evil act on the earth as it happened, every child being molested, beat, murdered, and every bad thing happening. That would not be heaven, because the Bible clearly says, no more tears, no more pain, no more sorrow. So I know without a doubt the best is yet to come for the children of God.

There is a place of total peace, in the grave for those of us, who die before His coming.

I am so excited to live for God, because He is my only hope in this life!

Heaven is so going to be worth it all!

I pray that you are a child of God, and not a sinner, when you stand before Him in judgment.

HEAVEN

"And I saw a new heaven and a new earth: for the first heaven and the first earth were passed away; and there was no more sea." (Revelation 21:1)

"Nevertheless we, according to his promise, look for new heavens and a new earth, wherein dwelleth righteousness." (2 Peter 3:13)

"But as it is written, Eye hath not seen, nor ear heard, neither have entered into the heart of man, the things which God hath prepared for them that love him." (1 Corinthians 2:9)

What a promise for the children of God! All of the old things are passed away, how wonderful heaven is going to be! We can not begin to imagine what heaven will be like.

"That the trial of your faith, being much more precious than of gold that perisheth, though it be tried with fire, might be found unto praise and honor and glory at the appearing of Jesus Christ:" (1 Peter 1:7)

"For the hope which is laid up for you in heaven, whereof ye heard before in the word of the truth of the gospel;" (Colossians 1:5)

"Looking for that blessed hope, and the glorious appearing of the great God and our Savior Jesus Christ;" (Titus 2:13)

"Enter ye in at the strait gate: for wide is the gate, and broad is the way, that leadeth to destruction, and many there be which go in thereat:" (Matthew 7:13)

"Because strait is the gate, and narrow is the way, which leadeth unto life, and few there be that find it." (Matthew 7:14)

"But now being made free from sin, and become servants to God, ye have your fruit unto holiness, and the end everlasting life." (Romans 6:22)

"Blessed are they that do his commandments, that they may have right to the tree of life, and may enter in through the gates into the city." (Revelation 22:14)

What a joyous time, when we do walk the strait and narrow, to hear Him say these words!

"His lord said unto him, Well done, thou good and faithful servant: thou hast been faithful over a few things, I will make thee ruler over many things: enter thou into the joy of thy lord." (Matthew 25:21)

This promise is only for them who have denied themselves and wholly lived for God.

"There remaineth therefore a rest to the people of God." (Hebrews 4:9)

"For he that is entered into his rest, he also hath ceased from his own works, as God did from his." (Hebrews 4:10)

"Let us labour therefore to enter into that rest, least any man fall after the same example of unbelief." (Hebrews 4:11)

"To them who by patient continuance in well doing seek for glory and honour and immortality, eternal life:" (Romans 2:7)

"But if the Spirit of him that raised up Jesus from the dead dwell in you, he that raised up Christ from the dead shall also quicken your mortal bodies by his Spirit that dwelleth in you." (Romans 8:11)

"And this is the will of him that sent me, that every one which seeth the Son, and believeth on him, may have everlasting life: and I will raise him up at the last day." (John 6:40)

"For the Lord himself shall descend from heaven with a shout, with the voice of the archangel, and with the trump of God: and the dead in Christ shall rise first:" (1 Thessalonians 4:16)

"Then we which are alive and remain shall be caught up together with them in the clouds, to meet the Lord in the air: and so shall we ever be with the Lord." (1 Thessalonians 4:17)

Here we see something very interesting. Not everyone is going to die a death in this life. It clearly says some will be caught up to meet Him in the air. I would love to be one that is changed in the air. What a day that is going to be for thee children of God, I can only imagine. We have so much to be thankful for, if we are truly living our lives according to His Word.

"Behold, I shew you a mystery; We shall not all sleep, but we shall all be changed," (1 Corinthians 15:51)

"In a moment, in the twinkling of an eye, at the last trump: for the trumpet shall sound, and the dead shall be raised incorruptible, and we shall be changed." (1 Corinthians 15:52)

"For this corruptible must put on incorruption, and this mortal must put on immortality." (1Corinthians 15:53)

"So when this corruptible shall have put on incorruption, and this mortal shall have put on immortality, then shall be brought to pass the saying that is written, Death is swallowed up in victory." (1Corinthians 15:54)

Can you imagine how wonderful this is going to be? Living for God and giving ourselves completely to Him, is so going to be worth it.

People are so unwilling to give up the ways of this world because Satan has blinded them into thinking that you can live any way you want.

But, if you're not careful, by the time you realize that you can't live just any way you want, it could be too late.

"I have fought a good fight, I have finished my course, I have kept the faith:" (2 Timothy 4:7)

"Henceforth there is laid up for me a crown of righteousness, which the Lord, the righteous judge, shall give me at that day: and to me only, but unto all them also that love his appearing." (2 Timothy 4:8)

"Rejoice, and be exceeding glad: for great is your reward in heaven: for so persecuted they the prophets which were before you." (Matthew 5:12)

"For the Son of man shall come in the glory of his Father with his angels; and then he shall reward every man according to his works." (Matthew 16:27)

"Knowing that of the Lord ye shall receive the reward of the inheritance: for ye serve the Lord Christ." (Colossians 3:24)

"For in the resurrection they neither marry, nor are given in marriage, but are as the angels of God in heaven." (Matthew 22:30)

"For when they shall rise from the dead, they neither marry, nor are given in marriage; but are as the angels which are in heaven." (Mark 12:25)

Wow! Look at these scriptures, we will be as the angels. That tells me, we will be nothing like we are now. Our minds do not really understand this. Our thinking will be totally different. We will know everything, by His revelations.

"For there is nothing covered, that shall not be revealed; neither hid, that shall not be known." (Luke 12:2)

So we will know all things in heaven. Everything done and said in secret will be made know before all men. Nothing will be hidden from God, or His children.

"Fear none of those things which thou shalt suffer: behold, the devil shall cast some of you into prison, that ye maybe tried; and ye shall have tribulation ten days: be thou faithful unto death, and I will give thee a crown of life." (Revelation 2:10)

"And when the chief Shepherd shall appear, ye shall receive a crown of glory that fadeth not away." (1 Peter 5:4)

"Behold, I come quickly: hold that fast which thou hast, that no man take thy crown." (Revelation 3:11)

"Blessed is the man that endureth temptation: for when he is tried, he shall receive the crown of life, which the Lord hath promised to them that love him." (James 1:12)

"Do ye not know that the saints shall judge the world? and if the world shall be judged by you, are ye unworthy to judge the smallest matters?" (1 Corinthians 6:2)

"For as the new heavens and the new earth, which I will make, shall remain before me, saith the Lord, so shall your seed and your name remain." (Isaiah 66:22)

"And it shall come to pass, that from one new moon to another, and from one sabbath to another, shall all flesh come to worship before me, saith the Lord." (Isaiah 66:23)

"And they shall go forth, and look upon the carcases of the men that have transgressed against me: for their worm shall not die, neither shall there fire be quenched; and they shall be and abhorring unto all flesh." (Isaiah 66:24)

"For now we see through a glass, darkly; but then face to face: now I know in part; but then shall I know even as also I am known." (1 Corinthians 13:12)

> *"Having made known unto us the mystery of his will, according to his good pleasure which he hath purposed in himself:"* (Ephesians 1:9)

The Word of God says, that we are like the angels, and that we are neither male nor female.

So, I truly do not believe that we will be known as a mother, father, sister, brother, or anything like that. But, I do believe we will be known as prayer warriors, worshippers, being faithful, peace keepers, and soul winners. I really believe this is what the scripture means. That is the only way that we can possibly be able to judge the world and want them punished. No way could anyone stand before a loved one and tell God to send them to hell, but seeing them only as souls who chose to not live for God. That is exactly what the children of God will do. You will not recognize loved ones as family. The children of God will only see each individual as a sinner they are.

This understanding really helps me to know that if a loved one dies lost, and I make it, I will never know that they are lost. This lets me know that the children of God will not be looking for anyone in heaven, our main attraction will be God himself. That is the only thing that is going to matter in heaven. I don't believe we will be fishing nor doing anything of this world. All the old things are become new. I don't believe we will eat the foods of this old world. Our minds just can't comprehend what heaven is like.

> *"For we brought nothing into this world, and it is certain we can carry nothing out."* (1 Timothy 6:7)

We did not bring anything into this world with us and we are not taking anything out. I don't understand people who put things in peoples' caskets. It isn't going anywhere, that's for sure. All things will burn in that day.

Heaven is going to be worth it all. Nothing in this world is worth missing heaven for! If you're not sure where you will spend eternity, it's time to search the Bible, and see what it takes to be ready.

Don't rely on what you hear, study His Word and know for yourself. Because it's that Word, that is going to judge each one of us.

Get ready, Jesus is coming!

A NOTE FROM THE AUTHOR

AFTER RESEARCHING ALL OF THESE SCRIPTURES, I have come to a hard realization about myself. Being raised in church all of your life, and then backsliding, I had in my mind that because of my mom's prayers and faith that her children would be saved, no matter what I did, God would not allow me to be lost.

I have come to the realization that no one can get me to heaven and no one can send me to hell. It is a personal decision by each individual where they spend eternity. My mom died believing that all of her children would be saved, but even if all of her children are not saved in the end, God did not fail her. And, now I understand that she will not know if any of her children are lost, because we will not be known that way.

I am so glad God did not give up on me and gave me another chance to live for Him. I do know, had it not been for my mom's prayer life and her walk with God, I would not be where I am today.

It is so important that we realize that it is a very personal decision on our part about where we spend eternity.

One thing I have seen from people is that they use the excuse of being hurt by others, to not live for God. That is something that we have to get past. Our confidence can only be in God, and not man. Man will let you down. So, I pray, that we can all get past our hurts and live for God simply because He is God.

About the Author

THERESA ANN CREWS FLATT was born May 24, 1960 in Blytheville, Arkansas to Charles and Frances Crews. Theresa is the youngest of four children. The first born is Brenda, the second born is, their only son, Charlie Jr., then Linda came along. Six years after Linda was born, Theresa joined the family. It was only twelve years that Theresa became the only child left in the home as everyone else had graduated and moved out.

Charles began to pastor a church in Blytheville around 1970, and Theresa was a big part of that. Selling door to door, to help raise money. And as she got older played the piano and sang in church.

Theresa graduated from Blytheville High School in May of 1978. Not long after finishing school, she began her family. Theresa is married to a wonderful man she met in Savannah, Tennessee, Jimmy Edward Flatt. They are blessed with three sons, Chris, Ronnie, and Blake. One daughter, Pamla. And nine grandsons and one granddaughter.

Theresa began writing songs in 1986. She has written thirteen songs in all, and several poems for family and friends.

Theresa now drives a school bus in Dyer County Tennessee, and absolutely loves her job.

Church is to this day, still a big part of Theresa's life. Her desire is that people see Christ in her life every day.

www.ingramcontent.com/pod-product-compliance
Lightning Source LLC
Chambersburg PA
CBHW020634130526
44591CB00043BA/668